Weight Watchers

One Pot
Meals

Lesley Waters

SIMON & SCHUSTER

A VIACOM COMPANY

First published in Great Britain by Simon and Schuster, 1999
A Viacom Company

Simon and Schuster UK Ltd
Africa House
64-78 Kingsway
London
WC2B 6SX

Weight Watchers and *1, 2, 3 Success 2000* are Trademarks of Weight Watchers International, Inc. and used under its control by Weight Watchers (U.K.) Ltd.

Design: Moore Lowenhoff
Front Cover design: Design in Mind
Typesetting: Stylize Digital Artwork
Photography: Steve Baxter
Styling: Marian Price
Food preparation: Jane Stevenson

Weight Watchers Publications Manager: Elizabeth Egan
Weight Watchers Publications Assistant: Celia Whiston

A CIP catalogue record is available from the British Library

ISBN 0 68485 156 3

Printed in Hong Kong

Pictured on the front cover: *Orange Lentils with Mediterranean Lamb (page 24)*

Pictured on the back cover: *Nectarine Smoothie (page 44)*

Recipe notes:
Egg size is medium, unless otherwise stated.
Fruit and vegetables are medium-sized, unless otherwise stated.
It is important to use proper measuring spoons, not cutlery, for spoon measures.
1 tablespoon = 15 ml; 1 teaspoon = 5 ml.
Dried herbs can be substituted for fresh ones, but the flavour may not always be as good. Halve the fresh-herb quantity stated in the recipe.

Ⓥ shows the recipe is suitable for vegetarians

Contents

Introduction

Cooking great-tasting food does not require masses of pots, pans and kitchen gadgets or hours of your time! Equally, a fit and trim shape does not mean you can't enjoy your food. It's just a matter of getting the balance right.

One Pot Meals is a modern approach to cooking great family meals with a minimum of fuss. They range from super soups which may be baked in the oven to sizzling salads, which can be whipped up in a wok in no time at all. Oven-roasting, steam-frying and grilling are all covered.

There are so many advantages to cooking one pot meals – they are straight-forward and simple to cook. Shopping and preparation are also a breeze and the end result leaves you with a delicious meal without a mountain of washing up!

If you get the balance right and follow the *1,2,3 Success 2000*™ Programme, you can enjoy your food and will be amazed by the family feasts which you can conjure up in one pot!

Special Cooking Method

Steam-frying

This method of cooking crops up frequently in *One Pot Cooking* and uses a non-stick pan to start to fry an ingredient, over a medium heat, until slightly coloured. Then a tablespoon of water is added, the heat is reduced slightly and the pan is covered immediately with a lid which creates steam in the pan and helps the cooking. This enables you to cook with a minimum amount of oil and maximise the flavours in your food.

Pots and Pans

One pot cooking requires only a few items of practical equipment:

- A frying-pan or large hob and oven-style shallow dish that is equally at home in the oven or on the hob.
- A non-stick wok with a lid for steam-frying, and for stews and soups.
- A chopping board and a sharp kitchen knife.

Super Soups

This chapter is not just for first courses – far from it! These soups are substantial, tasty meals in their own right. They are hearty with loads of flavour and texture, and they range from thick and creamy to spicy and chunky. Nothing is more warming or comforting than a hot bowl of soup and these recipes will satisfy you again and again.

Tomato and Basil Stew

An oven-baked chunky soup with crunchy garlic toasts.

Serves: 2
Preparation and cooking time: 35 minutes
Freezing: not recommended
Points per serving: 4
Total Points per recipe: 8
Calories per serving: 405

Ⓥ

2 teaspoons olive oil
1 onion, chopped
a pinch of sugar
1 bay leaf
1 beef tomato, chopped roughly
400 g (14 oz) canned chopped tomatoes in tomato sauce
1 small french stick, cut into 4 × 5 cm (2-inch) thick slices
1 garlic clove, peeled
2 tablespoons fresh basil leaves, torn roughly
salt and freshly ground black pepper

❶ Preheat the oven to Gas Mark 6/200°C/400°F.
❷ Heat the oil in a shallow hob and ovenproof dish. Add the onion, cover and steam-fry (see page 4) for 10 minutes or until softened. Stir in the sugar and bay leaf. Add the beef tomato and chopped tomatoes. Season well and bring to a simmer. Transfer to the oven for 10 minutes.

❸ Meanwhile lay the bread slices on a baking tray and toast in the oven for 6–7 minutes or until golden. Remove and lightly rub the warm toast with the garlic clove.
❹ Serve in a bowl and place the toasts in the soup at a vertical angle (two per person). Scatter over the basil and serve at once.

Chicken Goulash Soup with Potato Dumplings

Chicken with red pepper and aubergine topped with puffed cheesy dumplings makes a hearty and filling goulash.

Serves: 4
Preparation time: 30 minutes + 20 minutes cooking
Freezing: not recommended
Points per serving: 5½
Total Points per recipe: 22½
Calories per serving: 440

2 teaspoons olive oil or sunflower oil
1 onion, chopped
1 small aubergine, diced
1 red pepper, de-seeded and sliced thickly
4 boneless, skinless chicken thighs
1 teaspoon flour
1 tablespoon paprika
2 teaspoons coriander seeds, crushed
400 g (14 oz) canned chopped tomatoes in a rich tomato sauce
grated rind of 1 lemon
salt and freshly ground black pepper
For the dumplings:
60 g (2¼ oz) dried potato flakes
300 ml (½ pint) semi-skimmed milk or water
1 small egg, beaten
25 g (1 oz) self-raising flour
25 g (1 oz) mature Cheddar, grated
1 tablespoon parsley, chopped roughly

1 Heat the oil in a large non-stick frying-pan or wok. Add the onion, aubergine and red pepper. Cover and steam-fry over a medium heat for 6–8 minutes until well coloured.

2 Cover the thighs with non-pvc film and using a mallet or rolling pin, flatten out each chicken thigh until approximately 5 mm (¼-inch) thick. Remove the film and cut each thigh in half. Remove the lid and add the chicken to the pan. Stir-fry for 1 minute.

3 Stir in the flour, paprika and coriander seeds. Fry for a further 30 seconds.

4 Add the tomatoes and lemon rind and season well. Bring to the boil, cover, and cook over a medium heat for 20 minutes.

5 For the dumplings, make the potato flakes into a mash by following the directions on the packet. Use either semi-skimmed milk or water. Cool slightly and beat in the egg, self-raising flour and cheese. Season.

6 Roll the mixture into 8 small dumplings and place on top of the soup. Spoon a little of the hot sauce from the soup over each dumpling and sprinkle with parsley. Cover again and cook for a further ten minutes over a medium heat until the dumplings are puffed and the chicken is cooked.

Weight Watchers note: if water is used instead of milk in step 5, deduct 1 Point from the total Points.

Mexican Sweetcorn and Turkey Chilli Soup

This Mexican-style chilli is fabulous with a crunchy, fresh sweetcorn and coriander salsa.

Serves: 4
Preparation time: 15 minutes + 25 minutes cooking
Freezing: not recommended
Points per serving: 7
Total Points per recipe: 28
Calories per serving: 355

1 tablespoon olive or sunflower oil
1 large onion, chopped
500 g (1 lb 2 oz) lean minced turkey
2 teaspoons ground cumin
1 teaspoon ground coriander
500 ml (18 fl oz) tomato passata
425 g (15 oz) canned kidney beans, drained and rinsed
1 or 2 red chillies, chopped finely or 1–2 teaspoons chilli sauce
300 ml ($^1/_2$ pint) turkey or chicken stock
salt and freshly ground black pepper
For the salsa:
4 spring onions with green tops, sliced
1 small red pepper, diced
175 g (6 oz) canned sweetcorn kernels, drained
3 tablespoons fresh coriander leaves, chopped roughly

1 In a large non-stick frying-pan or wok, heat the oil. Add the onion and fry for 5 minutes until softened.

2 Add the turkey mince and fry for a further 3–4 minutes. Sprinkle over the cumin and coriander and fry for 30 seconds.

3 Stir in the passata, kidney beans and chilli and half the stock. Bring to the boil and season well.

Simmer the chilli for 20–25 minutes adding more stock gradually if the pan becomes too dry.

4 Meanwhile, combine all the salsa ingredients together in a bowl and set to one side.

5 To serve, ladle the chilli into 4 serving bowls and top each with a large spoonful of salsa. Serve at once.

Thick Pea Borsch

An unusual mint and carrot raita is stirred into this thick pea soup for a dynamite soup and salad combination!
Serve with hot, crunchy granary toast, remembering to add the extra Points.

Serves: 4
Preparation time: 10 minutes + 15 minutes cooking
Freezing: not recommended
Points per serving: $2^1/_2$
Total Points per recipe: 10
Calories per serving: 150

2 teaspoons olive oil or sunflower oil
1 onion, chopped roughly
500 g (1 lb 2 oz) frozen petit pois
a pinch of sugar
850 ml (1$^1/_2$ pints) vegetable stock
salt and freshly ground black pepper
For the raita:
150 ml ($^1/_4$ pint) low-fat plain yogurt

1 large carrot, peeled and grated
3 tablespoons mint leaves, chopped

❶ Heat the oil in a large non-stick frying-pan or wok. Add the onion, cover and steam-fry for 5 minutes until softened.

❷ Stir in the peas, sugar and vegetable stock. Season well and bring to the boil. Cover and simmer for 10–12 minutes.

❸ Meanwhile, in a bowl, combine all the raita ingredients together and season. Set to one side.

❹ Using a hand-held blender or liquidiser, whizz the soup until smooth. Ladle immediately into 4 serving bowls and swirl a spoonful of raita into each. Serve at once.

Mushroom, Bacon and Potato Chowder

This creamy bacon and mushroom chowder is delicious topped with fresh spinach and a squeeze of lemon juice.

Serves: 4
Preparation time: 15 minutes + 20 minutes cooking
Freezing: not recommended
Points per serving: $4^1/_2$
Total Points per recipe: $18^1/_2$
Calories per serving: 240

2 teaspoons olive oil or sunflower oil
3 rashers of lean smoked bacon, diced
1 large leek, sliced
450 g (1 lb) potatoes, scrubbed and diced coarsely

225 g (8 oz) small button mushrooms, trimmed
150 ml ($^1/_4$ pint) white wine
300 ml ($^1/_2$ pint) semi-skimmed milk
300 ml ($^1/_2$ pint) chicken stock
2 level tablespoons cornflour, mixed with a little water
115 g (4 oz) spinach leaves, shredded
juice of $^1/_2$ lemon
a pinch of dried nutmeg
freshly ground black pepper

❶ Heat the oil in a large non-stick frying-pan or wok. Add the bacon and leek and fry for 5 minutes.

❷ Add the potatoes and mushrooms and fry for a further minute.

❸ Stir in the wine, milk and stock and season with black pepper and a grating of nutmeg. Bring to the boil and stir in the cornflour mix. Reduce the heat and simmer for 15–20 minutes or until the potatoes are just cooked.

❹ Stir in the shredded spinach and simmer for 1 minute. Squeeze over the lemon juice and serve at once.

Thick Pea Borsch
Mushroom, Bacon and Potato Chowder

Stir It Up

The non-stick wok is a really useful piece of cooking equipment and well worth the investment. It's a great vessel for stirring up a myriad of fast, nourishing feasts in minutes and, of course, all in one pot. Remember, stir-fries don't always have to be oriental-style food; French and British-style dishes can also be swirled into life as you'll see in this chapter.

Cauliflower and Almond Madras

Cauliflower, chick-peas and coconut are the perfect combination in this vegetable curry. Serve with warm pitta breads for dunking and don't forget to count the extra Points.

Serves: 4
Preparation time: 15 minutes + 20 minutes cooking
Freezing: not recommended
Points per serving: $4^1/_2$
Total Points per recipe: $17^1/_2$
Calories per serving: 240

Ⓥ

2 teaspoons olive oil or sunflower oil
1 large onion, sliced
2 tablespoons Madras curry powder
1 teaspoon flour
2 tablespoons unsweetened desiccated coconut
600 ml (1 pint) hot vegetable stock
175 g (6 oz) potato, scrubbed and sliced thinly
350 g (12 oz) cauliflower florets
425 g (15 oz) canned chick-peas, drained and rinsed
15 g ($^1/_2$ oz) toasted flaked almonds
3 tablespoons parsley, chopped roughly
salt and freshly ground black pepper

❶ In a large non-stick frying-pan or wok, heat the oil. Fry the onion for 2–3 minutes until lightly browned. Add 1 tablespoon water, cover and steam-fry for 5 minutes until softened.
❷ Add the curry powder and flour and fry for 1 minute.

❸ Mix the desiccated coconut with the hot stock and stir into the pan. Simmer for 1 minute.
❹ Add the potato slices, cauliflower florets and chick-peas and season well. Stir together, cover and simmer for 20–25 minutes. Scatter over the almonds and parsley and serve.

Cauliflower and Almond Madras

Thai Prawns with Sugar-snap Peas

Serves: 4
Preparation time: 15 minutes + 20 minutes cooking
Freezing: not recommended
Points per serving: $4^1/_2$
Total Points per recipe: $17^1/_2$
Calories per serving: 325

2 teaspoons olive oil or sunflower oil
1 onion, chopped
1 tablespoon red Thai paste
225 g (8 oz) long-grain rice
600 ml (1 pint) vegetable stock
175 g (6 oz) sugar-snap peas, halved lengthways
100 ml ($3^1/_2$ fl oz) vegetable stock (optional)
200 g (7 oz) frozen cooked prawns, thawed

1 Heat the oil in a large non-stick frying-pan or wok. Add the onion, cover and steam-fry (see page 4) for 5 minutes until softened.

2 Add the Thai paste and rice and fry, stirring, for 1 minute. Pour in 600 ml (1 pint) stock, cover and simmer for 10 minutes.

3 Remove the lid and add the sugar-snap peas. Cover and simmer for a further 8–10 minutes until the rice and peas are cooked, adding up to 100 ml ($3^1/_2$ fl oz) stock if the pan becomes dry.

4 Stir through the cooked prawns and heat for 1 minute. Serve at once.

Variation: if you wish, frozen peas can be used instead of sugar-snap peas. The Points per serving will be 5 and the total Points per recipe will be $19^1/_2$.

Chinese Cod with Black Bean Sauce

Serves: 2
Preparation time: 15 minutes + 15 minutes cooking
Freezing: not recommended
Points per serving: $6^1/_2$
Total Points per recipe: $13^1/_2$
Calories per serving: 420

115 g (4 oz) thread egg noodles
1 teaspoon olive oil

2×115 g (4 oz) skinless, boneless chunky cod fillets
4 lettuce leaves (large outer leaves of a round lettuce)
1 orange, peeled and segmented
juice of 1 orange
5 tablespoons black bean sauce
freshly ground black pepper

1 Preheat the oven to Gas Mark 6/200°C/400°F. Soak the egg noodles in boiling water, following the instructions on the packet.

2 Meanwhile, lightly brush 2 large pieces of double-thickness tin foil (approximately 20 cm/8 inches square) with the oil and set to one side.

3 Season each cod fillet with pepper and wrap 2 lettuce leaves around each fillet. Divide the noodles in half and place a mound in the centre of each piece of tin foil. Top each mound with a wrapped cod fillet.

4 In a small bowl, combine the orange segments, orange juice and black bean sauce. Spoon this mixture equally over the fish.

5 Loosely wrap the foil parcels and place on a baking tray in the oven. Bake for 10–15 minutes until the fish is cooked.

6 To serve, place each parcel on a large dinner plate and take straight to the table.

Thai Prawns with Sugar-snap Peas
Chinese Cod with Black Bean Sauce

Broccoli, Chicken and Cashew Nut Stir-fry

The delicious combination of chicken and cashew nuts tastes even better with a twist of orange!

Serves: 4

Preparation and cooking time: 20 minutes

Freezing: not recommended

Points per serving: $7^1/_2$

Total Points per recipe: $29^1/_2$

Calories per serving: 425

175 g (6 oz) dried thin egg noodles

2 teaspoons olive oil or sunflower oil

1 bunch of spring onions, sliced lengthways

4 medium skinless, boneless chicken thighs,
    cut into strips

1 orange pepper, de-seeded and sliced

175 g (6 oz) broccoli florets

150 ml ($1/_4$ pint) orange juice

2 teaspoons cornflour mixed with 1 tablespoon
    water

2 tablespoons soy sauce

55 g (2 oz) cashew nuts

salt and freshly ground black pepper

❶ Soak the noodles in boiling water, following the directions on the packet. Meanwhile, in a large non-stick frying-pan or wok, heat the oil. Add the spring onions, cover and steam-fry (see page 4) for 2 minutes until softened.

❷ Add the chicken and orange pepper, cover and steam-fry for a further 5–6 minutes, over a medium heat, stirring occasionally. The chicken should be just cooked and lightly coloured.

❸ Add the broccoli, cover again and cook for 4–5 minutes. Stir in the orange juice, cornflour mix and soy sauce and season. Simmer for 1 minute. Stir in the cashew nuts and serve at once with the egg noodles.

Mustard Turkey with Green Beans

A chicken or turkey breast is complemented so well by this hot honey and mustard salad.
Delicious served with fresh crusty bread.

Serves: 4
Preparation and cooking time: 20 minutes
Freezing: not recommended
Points per serving: 3½
Total Points per recipe: 14
Calories per serving: 185

2 teaspoons olive oil or sunflower oil
350 g (12 oz) skinless, boneless turkey breast,
    cut into strips
juice of 1 lemon
3 tablespoons grainy mustard
2 tablespoons runny honey
115 g (4 oz) green beans, cut into 2 cm (³/₄-inch)
    pieces
1 tablespoon sesame seeds
salt and freshly ground black pepper
salad leaves, to serve

❶ In a large non-stick frying-pan or wok, heat the oil until very hot.

❷ In a bowl, toss together the turkey, lemon juice, mustard and honey. Season well.

❸ Add to the hot pan and stir-fry over a high heat for 3–4 minutes until the turkey is browned and nearly cooked.

❹ Stir in the beans and cook for a further 2–3 minutes. Sprinkle over the sesame seeds.

❺ Arrange the salad leaves on 4 individual serving dishes, spoon over the turkey and serve at once.

Spuds with Bacon and Spring Greens

This country-style dish with herby pan-fried new potatoes makes a complete meal.
Use new potatoes, scrub well and leave the skins on!

Serves: 3
Preparation time: 15 minutes + 25 minutes cooking
Freezing: not recommended
Points per serving: 4
Total Points per recipe: 11½
Calories per serving: 230

2 teaspoons olive or sunflower oil
1 red onion, cut into chunky strips
3 slices lean smoked bacon, diced
450 g (1 lb) new potatoes, halved lengthways
2 celery sticks, diced
300 ml (½ pint) vegetable stock
1 bay leaf
½ teaspoon dried mixed herbs
115 g (4 oz) spring greens, shredded
salt and freshly ground black pepper

❶ Heat the oil in a large non-stick frying-pan or wok. Add the onion, cover and steam-fry (see page 4) for 5 minutes. Add the bacon, potatoes and celery, cover again and steam-fry for 2 minutes.

❷ Stir in the stock, bay leaf and mixed herbs. Season. Cover and cook over a medium heat for 15–20 minutes until the potatoes are nearly cooked.

❸ Stir in the spring greens and toss together with the other ingredients. Cover again and cook for a further 5 minutes. Serve at once.

Nice Rice and Perfect Pasta

Pasta and rice make excellent store cupboard ingredients. These versatile staples are a great source of energy and can, at the drop of a hat, be rustled up into a filling and wholesome meal. As a rule, choose egg-free, dried pasta, since it contains less fat and always make a point of briefly rinsing your rice before cooking since this will remove any dust and improve the texture.

Fish Lasagne

Weight Watchers tasty soups make fantastic sauces. Here you can choose either Tomato or Mushroom soup to make quick fish lasagne!

Serves: 4

Preparation time: 5 minutes + 50 minutes cooking

Freezing: not recommended

Points per serving: 4

Total Points per recipe: with tomato soup $15^1/_2$; with mushroom soup 16

Calories per serving: 330

450 g (1 lb) frozen leaf spinach, thawed

450 g (1 lb) smoked haddock fillet, cut into chunks

2 × 295 g cans of Weight Watchers from Heinz Tomato or Mushroom soup

6 sheets, approximately 140 g (5 oz), no pre-cook lasagne

25 g (1 oz) breadcrumbs

25 g (1 oz) parmesan cheese, grated

freshly ground black pepper

1 Preheat the oven to Gas Mark 6/200°C/400°F.

2 Place half the spinach in the base of a large, shallow ovenproof dish. Top this with half the fish and then a quarter of the soup. Lay 3 sheets of lasagne on top. Season in between each layer with black pepper.

3 Next, layer on the remaining spinach, followed by the remaining fish and another quarter of the soup. Season and top with 3 more sheets of lasagne.

4 Pour over the remaining soup and lightly push down the lasagne sheets to ensure that all the lasagne is covered with soup. Sprinkle with the breadcrumbs and cheese.

5 Cover the lasagne with tin foil and bake for 35 minutes. Then remove the foil and cook for a further 10–15 minutes until browned and bubbling hot.

Roasted Vegetable Ragoût with Tagliatelle

Roasting root vegetables really intensifies their flavour and transforms the taste! Serve this ragoût topped with one of the many fresh, ready-made tomato salsas or pestos now available to buy.

Serves: 2

Preparation and cooking time: 40 minutes

Freezing: not recommended

Points per serving: if using salsa 5^1/$_2$; if using pesto 6^1/$_2$

Total Points per recipe: if using salsa 11; if using pesto 13

Calories per serving: if using salsa 515; if using pesto 530

Ⓥ

1 tablespoon olive oil

3 parsnips, diced

1 fennel bulb, diced

4 celery sticks, diced

1 onion, chopped roughly

3 large carrots, diced

600 ml (1 pint) herb stock

150 ml (^{1}/$_4$ pint) white wine

115 g (4 oz) quick-cook tagliatelle, broken up roughly

8 teaspoons ready-made tomato salsa or pesto, to serve

salt and freshly ground black pepper

❶ Preheat the oven to Gas Mark 6/200°C/400°F.

❷ Heat the oil in a hob and ovenproof pan. Add the parsnips, fennel, celery, onion and carrots. Fry for 2 minutes.

❸ Transfer the pan to the oven and bake, uncovered, for 20–25 minutes.

❹ Remove the pan from the oven and place back on the hob. Pour in the stock and wine, season and bring to the boil. Simmer for 2 minutes, then stir in the tagliatelle.

❺ Cover the pan and cook for a further 4–5 minutes or until the pasta is cooked. Serve the ragoût in individual bowls topped with 2 teaspoons each of fresh tomato salsa or fresh pesto.

Bubble and Squeak Pasta

This fantastic combination of smoked bacon and sun-dried tomatoes is sure to become a favourite!

Serves: 4
Preparation and cooking time: 30 minutes
Freezing: not recommended
Points per serving: 6
Total Points per recipe: 24
Calories per serving: 455

2 teaspoons olive oil
1 onion, chopped
3 rashers lean, smoked back bacon
1 garlic clove, peeled
2 teaspoons dried thyme
350 g (12 oz) dried rigatoni pasta
4 large sun-dried tomatoes, chopped
150 ml ($^1/_4$ pint) white wine
600 ml (1 pint) vegetable stock
100 ml ($3^1/_2$ fl oz) vegetable stock (optional)
115 g (4 oz) savoy cabbage, shredded
20 g ($^3/_4$ oz) parmesan cheese, grated
salt and freshly ground black pepper

❶ Heat the oil in a large non-stick frying-pan or wok. Add the onion and bacon. Fry for 5–6 minutes until the onion is softened and the bacon is lightly coloured.

❷ Add the garlic and thyme and fry for 1 minute. Stir in the pasta, sun-dried tomatoes, wine and 600 ml (1 pint) vegetable stock. Season well and cover. Cook over a medium heat for 12 minutes or until the pasta is cooked. Add a little more stock if the pan becomes too dry.

❸ 5 minutes before the end of the cooking time, stir in the shredded cabbage.

❹ To serve, sprinkle with the parmesan cheese, toss together and serve at once.

Variation: if you don't have rigatoni, any other dried pasta shapes or shells would work well too.

Orange Lentils with Mediterranean Lamb

Garlic and rosemary are the classic accompaniments for lamb. Add some orange lentils and brown rice and you have a hearty supper!

Serves: 4
Preparation time: 20 minutes + 40 minutes cooking
Freezing: not recommended
Points per serving: 7½
Total Points per recipe: 31
Calories per serving: 505

2 teaspoons olive oil
280 g (10 oz) leeks, sliced and washed

350 g (12 oz) lean lamb leg steak, cubed
2 garlic cloves, crushed
2 teaspoons dried rosemary
225 g (8 oz) easy-cook brown rice
115 g (4 oz) orange lentils, rinsed
1 yellow pepper, cut into strips (optional)
600 ml (1 pint) vegetable stock
300 ml (½ pint) vegetable stock (optional)
salt and freshly ground black pepper

❶ Heat the oil in large non-stick pan. Add the leeks, cover and steam-fry (see page 4) for 10 minutes until softened.

❷ Remove the lid, add the lamb, garlic and rosemary and fry for 2–3 minutes. Stir in the rice, lentils, yellow pepper and 600 ml (1 pint) of the stock. Season well and bring to the boil.

❸ Cover and simmer for 30–40 minutes until the rice is cooked. Stir occasionally and add more stock if the pan becomes too dry.

Kedgeree

Canned long-grain rice really speeds up this recipe for classic kedgeree.

Serves: 4
Preparation and cooking time: 15 minutes
Freezing: not recommended
Points per serving: with egg 6; without egg 5½
Total Points per recipe: with egg 24½; without egg 21½
Calories per serving: with egg 345; without egg 300

2 teaspoons olive oil or sunflower oil
1 onion, sliced

2 tablespoons mild curry paste
275 g (9½ oz) canned long-grain rice
300 ml (½ pint) vegetable stock
425 g (15 oz) canned red salmon, drained with the juice reserved
juice and grated rind of 1 lemon
3 tablespoons chopped fresh parsley
2 hard-boiled eggs, peeled and chopped (optional)
salt and freshly ground black pepper

❶ Heat the oil in a large non-stick frying-pan or wok. Add the onion and steam-fry (see page 4) for 5 minutes until softened. Add in the curry paste and cook for 30 seconds.

❷ Stir in the rice, stock and reserved salmon juice. Season. Cover and simmer for 3 minutes. Stir in the salmon and lemon juice. Heat through.

❸ Scatter over the lemon rind, parsley and chopped egg, if using, and serve at once.

Variation: tuna can be used instead of red salmon. The Points per serving will be 5 and the total Points per recipe will be 19½.

Orange Lentils with Mediterranean Lamb
Kedgeree

Baked Fruit Pilaff with Chicken

Baking whole lemon pieces really gets the most out of a lemon's flavour and juice. In this dish,
it makes a delicious sauce for the chicken and rice.

Serves: 2
Preparation time: 20 minutes + 35 minutes cooking
Freezing: not recommended
Points per serving: 8¹/₂
Total Points per recipe: 17¹/₂
Calories per serving: 575

2 teaspoons olive oil or sunflower oil
1 onion, chopped
¹/₂ teaspoon cumin
¹/₂ teaspoon ground coriander
¹/₂ teaspoon cinnamon
1 teaspoon turmeric
1 garlic clove, crushed
175 g (6 oz) long-grain rice
25 g (1 oz) sultanas
55 g (2 oz) dried, ready-to-eat prunes, chopped roughly
450 ml (16 fl oz) vegetable stock
¹/₂ lemon, cut in half
2 small chicken breasts
1 teaspoon honey
salt and freshly ground black pepper

❶ Preheat the oven to Gas Mark 6/200°C/400°F.

❷ Heat the oil in a hob and oven-proof dish. Add the onion and fry for 5 minutes. Add the spices and fry for a further 30 seconds. Stir in the garlic, rice, sultanas, prunes and vegetable stock. Squeeze over the juice from the lemon pieces, then add the lemon pieces to the pan.

❸ Season well and bring the contents of the pan to the boil. Simmer for 1 minute, then cover and transfer to the oven for 15 minutes.

❹ Cover the chicken with non-pvc film and using a mallet or rolling pin, flatten out the chicken breasts until they are approximately 1 cm (¹/₂-inch) thick.

Using a sharp knife, cut each breast in half and score each piece in a criss-cross pattern, taking care not to cut all the way through the chicken breast. Season and set to one side.

❺ Drizzle the scored chicken pieces with the honey. Remove the dish from the oven and place the chicken pieces on the rice, pushing them down slightly into the surface of the rice. Use 2 teaspoons to carefully pick up the cooked lemon pieces in the pan and squeeze out any remaining lemon juice over the chicken and rice.

❻ Return the dish to the oven for 15–20 minutes until the chicken is cooked.

Sizzling Salads

Gone are the days of the cold and dull salad plate, full of limp lettuce and acid beetroot. Salads are delicious, substantial meals in the main and can be served all the year round with a wide variety of exciting and interesting ingredients. In this chapter, vegetables, fish, meat and grains are used to create tasty dishes which can be served cold or sizzling hot, tossed in a flavoursome dressing.

Caesar and Roasted Potato Salad

Weight Watchers mayonnaise-style dressing keeps the Points low but really enhances the delicious flavours of roasted new potatoes and bacon.

Serves: 2
Preparation and cooking time: 25 minutes
Freezing: not recommended
Points per serving: 6
Total Points per recipe: 12
Calories per serving: 270

550 g (1 lb 4 oz) canned, unpeeled new potatoes, drained and rinsed (and halved if large)
1/2 red onion, sliced
1 rasher of lean, smoked back bacon, cut into thin strips
1 tablespoon olive oil
3 tablespoons Weight Watchers from Heinz mayonnaise-style dressing
juice of 1 lemon
1 small garlic clove, crushed
1 small cos lettuce or romaine lettuce
2 tablespoons chives, chopped roughly
freshly ground black pepper

1 Preheat the oven to Gas Mark 6/200°C/400°F.

2 In a non-stick roasting tin, toss together the new potatoes, onion, bacon and oil. Season with black pepper. Roast in the oven for 15–20 minutes.

3 Meanwhile, combine the mayonnaise-style dressing with the juice of 1/2 the lemon. Add the garlic and season with black pepper.

4 Reserve some of the large outer leaves of the lettuce and shred the remainder.

5 Toss the dressing with the hot potato mixture. Using the large lettuce leaves as a shell, pile in some of the shredded lettuce. Top with the hot potato mixture and squeeze over a little extra lemon juice. Sprinkle with the chives and serve at once.

Baked Roasted Vegetables with Hummous Toasts

Baking gives an intensely sweet flavour to these colourful vegetables. Serve with low-fat hummous and sesame toasts for a memorable feast!

Serves: 4
Preparation time: 5 minutes + 50 minutes cooking
Freezing: not recommended
Points per serving: 3
Total Points per recipe: 11½
Calories per serving: 220

Ⓥ

2 courgettes, cut into 2.5 cm (1-inch) chunks
1 large aubergine, cut into 2.5 cm (1-inch) chunks
1 red pepper, cut into 2.5 cm (1-inch) chunks
1 yellow pepper, cut into 2.5 cm (1-inch) chunks
2 red onions, cut into wedges
1 tablespoon olive oil
2 tablespoons fresh thyme
50 ml (2 fl oz) herb vegetable stock
75 ml (2¾ oz) herb vegetable stock (optional)
2 tablespoons balsamic vinegar
4 medium slices of country-style bread
4 tablespoons low-fat hummous
2 teaspoons toasted sesame seeds
salt and freshly ground black pepper

❶ Preheat the oven to Gas Mark 6/200°C/400°F.
❷ In a non-stick roasting pan, toss all the vegetables together with the oil and thyme. Season well and pour over 50 ml (2 fl oz) of the stock. Bake the vegetables in the oven for 50–60 minutes until tender and slightly browned. Add up to 75 ml (2¾ fl oz) more stock if the roasting tin becomes too dry.

❸ Remove from the oven and stir in the balsamic vinegar.
❹ Place the bread slices in the oven to toast. Spread each toasted slice with some hummous and sprinkle with the toasted sesame seeds. Serve the warm roasted vegetables with the hummous toasts.

Baked Roasted Vegetables with Hummous Toasts
Caesar and Roasted Potato Salad (page 27)

Tomato, Mint and Lentil Salad

Canned lentils are a wonderful and quick alternative to the dried ones. Hot and Spicy Croûtes (below) are delicious with this.

Serves: 4
Preparation and cooking time: 20 minutes
Freezing: not recommended
Points per serving: $2^1/_2$
Total Points per recipe: 11
Calories per serving: 130

2 teaspoons olive oil
1 large onion, diced
1 rasher of lean smoked back bacon, diced
200 ml (7 fl oz) tomato passata
425 g (15 oz) canned green lentils, drained and rinsed
2 tablespoons roughly chopped fresh mint
115 g (4 oz) cherry tomatoes, halved
4 thick slices of iceberg lettuce
salt and freshly ground black pepper

❶ Heat the oil in a non-stick frying-pan. Add the onion and bacon and fry gently for 10 minutes until softened and lightly coloured.

❷ Add the tomato passata to the pan and season well. Simmer for 2 minutes.

❸ Add the lentils and mint and toss together well. Carefully stir in the cherry tomatoes.

❹ Place a slice of iceberg lettuce on each serving plate and pile the salad on top to serve.

Hot and Spicy Croûtes

These are the perfect accompaniment to tomato, mint and lentil salad and many other dishes!

Serves: 4
Preparation and cooking time: 10 minutes
Freezing: not recommended
Points per serving: 1
Total Points per recipe: 5
Calories per serving: 80

8×1 cm ($^1/_2$-inch) thick slices of French stick
2 teaspoons olive oil
$^1/_4$ teaspoon ground cumin
$^1/_4$ teaspoon ground coriander
$^1/_4$ teaspoon paprika

Ⓥ

❶ Preheat the oven to Gas Mark 6/200°C/400°F.

❷ Brush the bread on each side with a little oil and place on a baking sheet.

❸ In a bowl, toss the spices together and sprinkle over the top side of the bread.

❹ Bake in the oven for 5–8 minutes until toasted and golden. Serve warm.

Spiced Turkey Salad Tortillas

Serves: 4

Preparation and cooking time: 25 minutes
+ 1 hour marinating

Freezing: not recommended

Points per serving: 5$^{1}/_{2}$

Total Points per recipe: 22$^{1}/_{2}$

Calories per serving: 280

250 g (9 oz) turkey breast
1 onion, cut into wedge-like strips
1 tablespoon olive oil
juice of 1 lemon
1 teaspoon hot chilli powder
2 teaspoons ground cumin
salt and freshly ground black pepper

To serve:
4 large flour tortillas
4 handfuls of crunchy salad leaves, shredded
1 small red pepper, cut into strips
115 g (4 oz) canned baby sweetcorn, drained
and rinsed
2 tablespoons low-fat plain yogurt
lime wedges

❶ Cover the turkey with non-pvc film and with a mallet or rolling pin, flatten the turkey until it is thin and then cut it into rough pieces. In a large bowl, toss together the turkey, onion, $^{1}/_{2}$ tablespoon oil, lemon juice, chilli powder and cumin. Season and set to one side to marinate for an hour.

❷ Warm the tortillas according to the packet instructions. Meanwhile, heat the remaining $^{1}/_{2}$ tablespoon oil in a non-stick frying-pan. Pour in the turkey mixture with all its marinade and fry for 2 minutes. Cover the pan with a lid and simmer for 4–5 minutes, until the turkey is cooked.

❸ To serve, allow each person to place some crisp salad leaves, red pepper and baby sweetcorn on a warm tortilla. Top each one with some spiced turkey and a blob of yogurt. Squeeze some lime juice over each and wrap up to eat. Garnish each plate with a lime wedge.

Warm Cannellini Salad with Beetroot Relish (page 34)
Spiced Turkey Salad Tortillas

Warm Cannellini Salad with Beetroot Relish

This fabulous bean and beetroot combination tastes best when piled on to warm crusty bread!

Serves: 4

Preparation and cooking time: 5 minutes
+ 1 hour marinating

Freezing: not recommended

Points per serving: 5

Total Points per recipe: $19^1/_2$

Calories per serving: 280

1 tablespoon olive oil
4 celery sticks, diced (leaves reserved for garnish)
6 large spring onions with green tops, sliced
1 large garlic clove, crushed
85 ml (3 fl oz) herb stock
800 g (1 lb 12 oz) canned cannellini beans, drained and rinsed
200 g (7 oz) canned skinless, boneless red salmon, flaked roughly
2 tablespoons low-fat fromage frais
salt and freshly ground black pepper
celery leaves, to garnish
For the beetroot relish:
200 g (7 oz) cooked beetroot, diced
juice of $^1/_2$ lemon
1 teaspoon sugar
1 teaspoon coriander seeds, crushed
2 tablespoons flat-leaf parsley, chopped roughly

1 To make the hot dressing, heat the oil in a non-stick pan. Add the celery and fry gently for 5 minutes. Add the spring onions and garlic and fry for a further minute. Pour in the stock and season well. Simmer for 1 minute.

2 Place the cannellini beans in a large bowl. Pour over the hot dressing and gently toss together. Set aside to marinate for an hour.

3 Combine all the ingredients for the relish together, season well and set to one side.

4 To serve, gently stir the salmon into the dressed cannellini beans. Spoon into four serving bowls and top each with some of the beetroot relish. Top with a blob of fromage frais, add the celery leaves and serve at once.

Crust and Crumb

This chapter will enable you to make fresh, savoury pies and crumbles which aren't laden with greasy pastry and unwanted Points and Calories. Ranging from a tasty Thai chicken crumble to a herby upside-down pizza, these dishes offer a wide variety of flavours and textures which the whole family can enjoy.

Smoked Mackerel and Horseradish Bread Pudding

A savoury version of a traditional pud!

Serves: 3
Preparation time: 10 minutes + 30 minutes standing + 30 minutes cooking
Freezing: not recommended
Points per serving: $9^1/_2$
Total Points per recipe: 29
Calories per serving: 710

3 large slices of granary bread, quartered
225 g (8 oz) skinless, boneless peppered
    mackerel fillets, flaked
2 eggs
425 ml (15 fl oz) skimmed milk
3 tablespoons low-fat milk powder
2 tablespoons horseradish, to taste
To serve:
crisp salad leaves
1 lemon, cut into wedges

❶ Lay the bread quarters in a 1.7 litre (3 pint) shallow ovenproof dish. Scatter over the flaked mackerel.

❷ In a bowl, whisk together the eggs, milk, milk powder and horseradish. Pour this over the bread and mackerel and set to one side to stand for 30 minutes.

❸ Preheat the oven to Gas Mark 5/190°C/375°F.

❹ Bake for approximately 30 minutes until puffed, firm and lightly golden. Serve at once with the crisp salad leaves. Place a lemon wedge on each plate and squeeze over the dish.

Green Thai Chicken Crumble

Be careful when adding the Thai paste as some brands can be very spicy!

Serves: 4 (for lunch) or 2 (for dinner)
Preparation and cooking time: 40 minutes
Freezing: not recommended
Points per serving: 5½ for 4; 11 for 2
Total Points per recipe: 22
Calories per serving: 300

2 teaspoons sunflower oil
1 onion, chopped
4 skinless, boneless chicken thighs, diced into
   2.5 cm (1 inch) pieces
3 teaspoons green Thai paste (or to taste)
4 level teaspoons flour
300 ml (½ pint) semi-skimmed milk
300 ml (½ pint) chicken stock
225 g (8 oz) broccoli florets
115 g (4 oz) frozen peas
40 g (1½ oz) breadcrumbs (made with 1-day-old
   bread)
1 tablespoon unsweetened desiccated coconut
salt and freshly ground black pepper

1 Preheat the oven to Gas Mark 6/200°C/400°F.

2 Heat the oil in a large and shallow non-stick pan. Add the onion, cover and steam-fry (see page 4) for 5 minutes. Add the chicken, cover and steam-fry for a further 3 minutes. Remove the lid and add the Thai paste. Fry for 30 seconds, then stir in the flour and fry for a further 30 seconds.

3 Remove the pan from the heat and gradually stir in the milk and chicken stock. Season well and return to the heat. Bring to the boil, stirring occasionally and simmer for 8 minutes.

4 Add the broccoli florets to the pan, cover and simmer for 2 minutes. Then add the peas and simmer for a further 2 minutes.

5 Meanwhile, in a bowl, combine the breadcrumbs with the desiccated coconut. Sprinkle this mix over the surface of the Thai chicken and transfer the uncovered pan to the oven for 10–12 minutes until the crumble is lightly browned.

Mixed Bean and Chilli Con Carne Pie

Taco shells provide a deliciously crunchy topping for this bean pie.

Serves: 4
Preparation time: 15 minutes + 30 minutes cooking
Freezing: not recommended
Points per serving: 8¹/₂
Total Points per recipe: 33¹/₂
Calories per serving: 370

2 teaspoons sunflower oil
1 onion, chopped
450 g (1 lb) lean minced pork
2 teaspoons cumin
1 garlic clove
425 g (15 oz) canned borlotti beans, drained
    and rinsed
200 g (7 oz) canned kidney beans, drained
    and rinsed
400 ml (14 fl oz) tomato passata
300 ml (¹/₂ pint) vegetable stock
3 taco shells, broken up coarsely
25 g (1 oz) reduced-fat Cheddar, grated
salt and freshly ground black pepper

❶ Preheat the oven to Gas Mark 5/190°C/375°F.

❷ Heat the oil in a dish which can go on the hob and in the oven. Add the onion and fry for five minutes until softened. Stir in the pork, cumin and garlic. Fry, stirring, for a further 2–3 minutes.

❸ Stir in the borlotti and kidney beans, tomato passata and stock. Season well. Bring to a simmer and remove from the heat. Scatter over the bits of taco shells and grated cheese and immediately transfer to the oven. Bake for 30 minutes until bubbling hot.

Variation: for a change, leave the taco shells whole and fill with the baked chilli.

Greek Lamb and Vegetable Flat Strudel

This flat strudel is layered rather than rolled. It is quick and simple to prepare with a light, crisp result!

Serves: 4

Preparation time: 5 minutes + 30 minutes standing + 40 minutes cooking

Freezing: not recommended

Points per serving: $7^1/_2$

Total Points per recipe: 29

Calories per serving: 335

1 onion, diced

1 large courgette, diced

2 teaspoons dried oregano

2 garlic cloves, crushed

juice of 1 lemon

350 g (12 oz) lean minced lamb

5 tablespoons vegetable purée

8 sheets of filo pastry, approximately 200 g (7 oz)

2 tablespoons skimmed milk

1 egg, beaten

1 teaspoon sesame seeds

salt and freshly ground black pepper

❶ In a bowl, combine the onion, courgette, oregano, garlic and lemon juice. Set to one side for 30 minutes.

❷ Preheat the oven to Gas Mark 5/190°C/375°F.

❸ Add the lamb and the vegetable purée to the vegetable mixture above and mix together. Season well.

❹ On a non-stick baking sheet, layer up 4 sheets of the filo pastry, lightly brushing each sheet with 1 tablespoon of skimmed milk. Carefully spread the lamb and vegetable mixture evenly over the pastry. Top with the remaining 4 sheets of filo and lightly brush between each sheet with the remaining skimmed milk.

❺ Brush the top of the pie with the beaten egg, and using a sharp knife, cut through the top layer in a criss-cross fashion. Sprinkle over the sesame seeds and bake for 40–45 minutes until golden brown and cooked.

Roast Chicken with Carrot and Poppyseed Stuffing

Sunday lunch with all the trimmings!

Serves: 4

Preparation time: 15 minutes + 2 hours cooking

Freezing: not recommended

Points per serving: 4½

Total Points per recipe: 17½

Calories per serving: 495

1.3 kg (3 lb) roasting chicken

2 lemons, halved

1 bay leaf

4 large garlic cloves

12 very small potatoes approximately 50 g (1¾ oz) each, washed well

150 ml (¼ pint) herb or vegetable stock

salt and freshly ground black pepper

For the stuffing:

115 g (4 oz) fresh breadcrumbs

1 large carrot, grated

3 teaspoons poppyseeds

1 onion, grated

grated zest and juice of 1 small orange

1 celery stick, chopped very finely

1 egg white, beaten

❶ Preheat the oven to Gas Mark 6/200°C/400°F.

❷ Using sharp kitchen scissors, remove the backbone from the chicken. Pull the chicken open slightly and lay the chicken, skin-side down, in a large roasting tin. Squeeze over the juice of 1 lemon and place the squeezed halves in the upturned cavity along with the bay leaf. Season well and roast in the oven for 40 minutes.

❸ Meanwhile, combine all the stuffing ingredients in a bowl and season well.

❹ Carefully lift the chicken out of the roasting tin after it has roasted for 40 minutes and transfer to a plate, skin-side up. Drain off any fat from the tin and, using your hands, place the stuffing in a mound, approximately the size of the chicken cavity, on the base of the tin.

❺ Take the chicken and place it skin-side up on top of the stuffing. Season again and squeeze over the juice from the remaining lemon halves. Surround the chicken with the garlic cloves, potatoes and squeezed lemon halves. Pour in the stock.

❻ Return to the oven for a further 60 – 90 minutes, until the potatoes are cooked and the chicken juices run clear.

Upside-down Pizza Pie

This tasty pizza is full of flavour – roasted peppers with garlic and cheese are a truly wonderful combination.

Serves: 4

Preparation time: 40 minutes + 15 minutes cooking

Freezing: not recommended

Points per serving: with low-fat soft cheese $4^1/_2$; with low-fat fromage frais 3; with low-fat quark 3

Total Points per recipe: with low-fat soft cheese $13^1/_2$; with low-fat fromage frais $12^1/_2$; with low-fat quark $11^1/_2$

Calories per serving: with low-fat soft cheese 205; with low-fat fromage frais 175; with low-fat quark 185

Ⓥ if using vegetarian cheese

1 tablespoon olive oil

2 red peppers, de-seeded and halved

1 orange pepper, de-seeded and halved

1 yellow pepper, de-seeded and halved

1 large red onion, cut into wedge-like strips

145 g packet of pizza base mix

1 large garlic clove, crushed

1 teaspoon dried mixed herbs

115 g (4 oz) low-fat soft cheese, fromage frais or quark

salt and freshly ground black pepper

❶ Preheat the oven to Gas Mark 6/200°C/400°F.

❷ Rub the oil over the base of a shallow and round baking tin, approximately 24 cm ($9^1/_2$ inches) in diameter. Lay the pepper halves on the base, skin-side down and scatter over the onion strips. Season well.

❸ Bake in the oven for 25 minutes until the peppers are slightly charred.

❹ Meanwhile, make up the pizza dough as directed on the packet, kneading in the crushed garlic. Roll out into a large, thin circle, large enough to cover the peppers.

❺ Remove the lightly charred peppers from the oven and sprinkle with the mixed herbs. Take the circle of dough and lay it over the peppers and onions. Return the pizza pie to the oven for a further 12–15 minutes until the dough is risen and golden.

❻ Remove from the oven and turn the pizza out, upside-down, on to a large serving plate or board. Place blobs of the cheese over the peppers and serve at once.

Pudding Pots

Puddings don't have to be complicated or full of fat to taste great. Just try the recipes for Chocolate Mousse and Hot Strawberry Cream Trifle and you'll see how true it is. All these scrumptious puds can be made with very little time and effort so you can whip them up on a whim if you fancy something a little indulgent.

Not-so-naughty Chocolate Mousse

Serves: 4

Points per serving: 4

Total Points per recipe: 17

Calories per serving: 240

Simmer 175 g (6 oz) pre-soaked prunes in a little water until very soft. Transfer to a processor and blend until smooth. In a bowl, whisk 3 egg whites until stiff, then whisk in 3 teaspoons caster sugar until thick and glossy. Lightly fold together the puréed prunes, whisked eggs and sugar and 115 g (4 oz) melted chocolate. Transfer the chocolate mousse to 4 individual serving glasses and chill until required.

Nectarine Smoothie

Serves: 2

Points per serving: 2

Total Points per recipe: 4$^{1}/_{2}$

Calories per serving: 105

In a food processor or liquidiser, place 2 large, ripe stoned nectarines, 1 large peeled orange, 50 ml (2 fl oz) water and a squeeze of lemon juice. Whizz until smooth. Pour into 2 soup bowls, swirl a tablespoonful of low-fat plain fromage frais over each. Roughly smash a ready-made meringue nest and top each smoothie with some crumbled meringue and a spoonful of canned raspberries.

Not-so-naughty Chocolate Mousse
Nectarine Smoothie

Tropical Parcels

Serves: 4
Points per serving: 3

Total Points per recipe: 12$^1/_2$
Calories per serving: 245

Preheat the oven to Gas Mark 6/200°C/400°F. Use 400 g (14 oz) canned drained mango slices, juice reserved, 400 g (14 oz) canned drained lychees and 1 large sliced ripe banana. Divide the fruits between 4 double thickness squares of tin foil approximately 15 cm (6 inches) square, placing them in the centre of each square. Spoon 1 tablespoon of the reserved mango juice over each and top with a fresh lime wedge. Enclose the parcels and bake in the oven for 10–15 minutes. Squeeze over the hot lime and serve with a 60 g (2$^1/_4$ oz) scoop of Weight Watchers from Heinz Iced Vanilla Dessert.

Hot Strawberry Cream Trifle

Serves: 2
Points per serving: 5

Total Points per recipe: 10
Calories per serving: 135

Gently heat the juice of a large orange with 115 g (4 oz) quartered strawberries. Take 2 serving glasses and roughly crumble 3 sponge fingers into the base of each. Top with a generous spoonful of Weight Watchers from Heinz Iced Vanilla Dessert. Spoon over the hot strawberries with all their juice and add a sprig of mint.

Blackened Baked Banana with Cream and Maple

Serves: 1
Points per serving: 2$^1/_2$
Ⓥ if using gelatine-free crème fraîche

Total Points per recipe: 2$^1/_2$
Calories per serving: 155

Preheat the oven to Gas Mark 6/200°C/400°F. Place a large banana on a baking tray and bake in the oven for 12–15 minutes until blackened. Remove and cut down the side to split open. Spoon 2 teaspoons of low-fat crème fraîche into the split and drizzle over a teaspoon of maple syrup or a little runny honey.

Instant Iced Berries

Serves: 4
Points per serving: 1

Total Points per recipe: 3$^1/_2$
Calories per serving: 60

Take a 450 g (1 lb) bag of frozen berry fruit mix and thaw slightly. Place in a food processor with approximately 2 teaspoons icing sugar. Whizz briefly, add 2 tablespoons Greek-style yogurt and whizz again briefly. Serve at once!

Instant Iced Berries
Blackened Baked Banana with Cream and Maple

Index